CAN WE LIVE ON MARS?

Astronomy for Kids 5th Grade Children's Astronomy & Space Books

Speedy Publishing LLC
40 E. Main St. #1156
Newark, DE 19711
www.speedypublishing.com
Copyright 2017

In this book, we're going to talk about whether or not people will be able to live on Mars someday. So, let's get right to it!

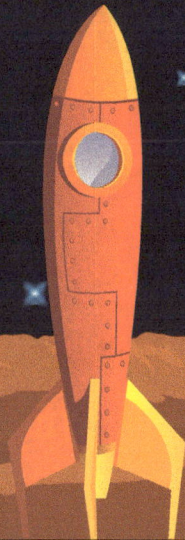

CAN WE LIVE ON MARS?

Scientists believe that the planet Mars may once have had an atmosphere. They also think that it had plenty of liquid water. However, these conditions existed billions of years ago and they're not true now. Currently, it would be next to impossible for human beings to live on Mars for any length of time.

Planet Mars at Sunrise

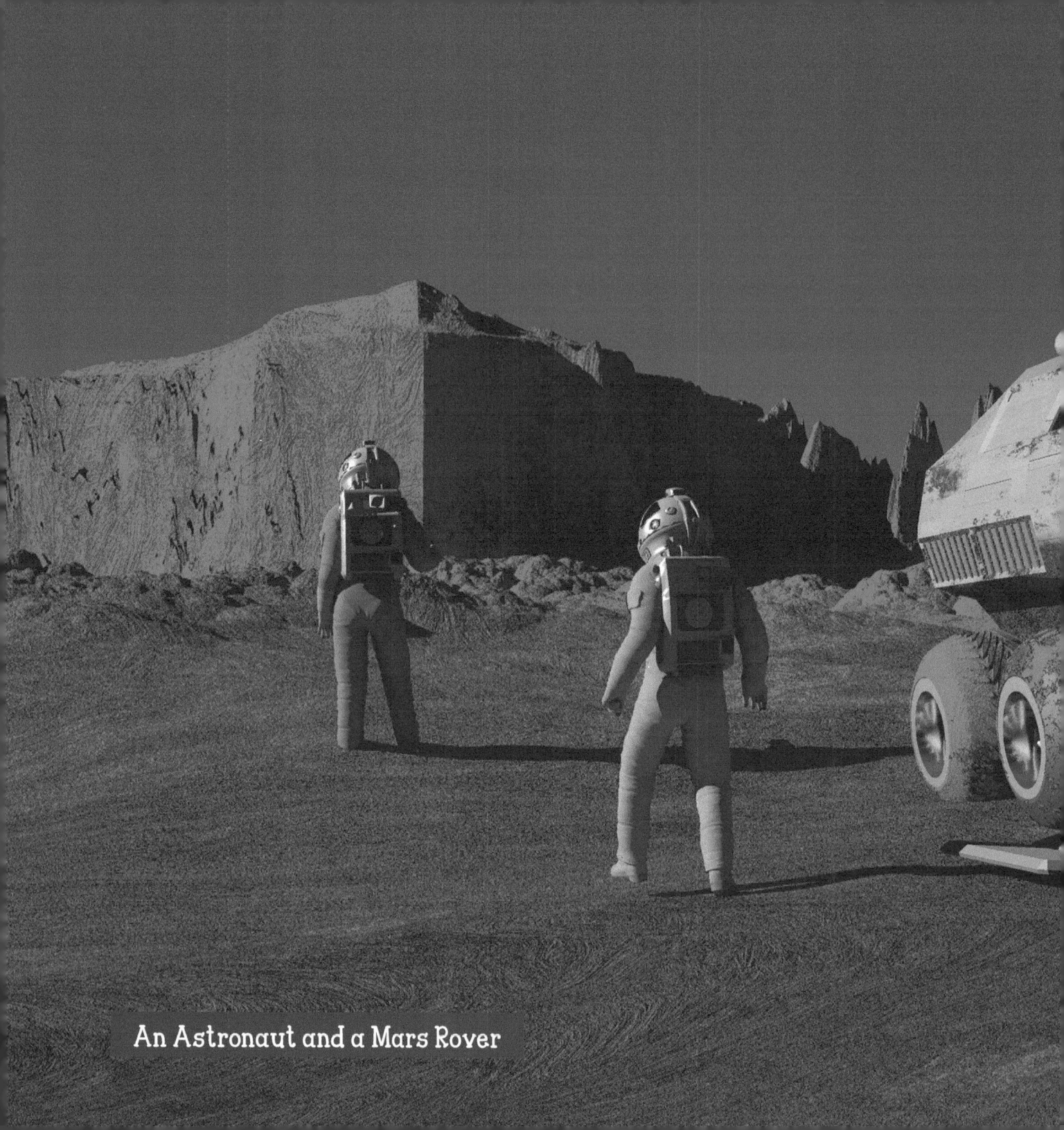
An Astronaut and a Mars Rover

It doesn't have an atmosphere that we can breathe. It has a surface temperature with extremes of very cold to moderately cold. Due to its lack of atmosphere, it gets bombarded by the intense radiation from the sun. On Earth, we're shielded from these dangerous rays by our atmosphere and magnetic field.

Landscape on the Planet Mars

So the short answer is no, we can't currently live on Mars. However, that doesn't mean that Mars couldn't be changed to make it possible for people to live there. Human beings have always been wanderers. We've always been looking for new places to explore and new places to live. If we want to be travelers and eventually see other places within our universe, Mars is the closest "neighborhood" in our solar system to visit. It's closer to an environment that is suitable than any of the other planets are.

REASONS TO GO TO MARS

There are many possible reasons why people want to travel to Mars. Here are some of the reasons why planning this trip is a good idea.

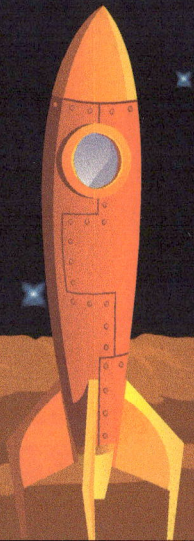

We want to:

- ➲ Explore a "new world"
- ➲ Create another place to go, in case something happens to Earth
- ➲ Discover resources like precious metals or minerals
- ➲ Learn the process of colonizing another planet
- ➲ Build a location that's a "stepping stone" to other space exploration
- ➲ Conquer a difficult goal that will be an achievement for humanity

Planet Mars

Elon Musk, the billionaire who is the CEO of Tesla Motors is also the head of another transportation company called SpaceX. His company is designing rockets, rovers, and other types of equipment to support this journey. He thinks that mankind should work toward getting the infrastructure ready on Mars for a colony of about a million people.

REASONS NOT TO GO TO MARS

- ➲ Although it's a worthy vision of the future, there are also a lot of reasons not to go to Mars.
- ➲ There's no oxygen. The very thin atmosphere is mostly carbon dioxide.
- ➲ There's no air pressure.
- ➲ The temperatures vary from -190 degrees Fahrenheit to 60 degrees Fahrenheit. In other words, it's mostly very frigid.
- ➲ The radiation that hits the surface is deadly to humans.
- ➲ There's almost no liquid water. Any water or ice that is available would have way too much salt content to be drinkable without processing.

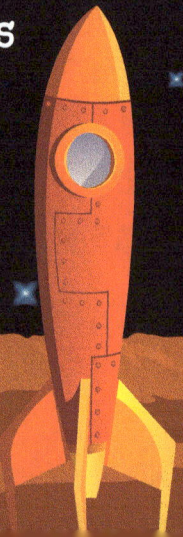

Planet Mars and Moon

Mars

- The soil is toxic because it contains a great deal of salt percholate. The salt percholate would need to be removed before crops could be grown.

- There are huge dust storms on Mars.

- Spare parts and medical supplies would have to come from Earth on a regular basis. This flow of needed materials from Earth would mean long delays between drops. It would also be very expensive.

- Mars only has about 40% of the gravity of Earth. It's not known how this change in gravity will affect human bodies over time.

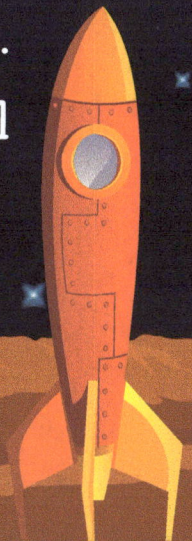

It's clear that we would need a lot of sophisticated technology to survive on Mars for a long time.

Mars Surface

Mars Surface

POSSIBLE SOLUTIONS PROPOSED BY SCIENTISTS

To survive the air pressure conditions and the cold temperatures, humans will need environments that are artificially pressurized and heated. They'll also need appropriate spacesuits whenever they go out of their controlled environments. Every hour outdoors will mean exposure to deadly radiation.

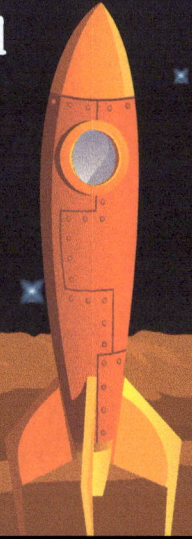

Humans living on Mars will need to figure out how to get drinkable water from the water that's frozen underground. Generating oxygen from the water so that the resulting air is breathable, and finding ways to make fuel for rockets from materials already available on the planet, will be top priorities too.

Mars Landscape

Earth and Mars

Growing food from the soil on Mars will be vitally important because shipping food from Earth wouldn't be practical in terms of both time and expense. NASA has done extensive experiments with hydroponics so it's possible to grow food on Mars.

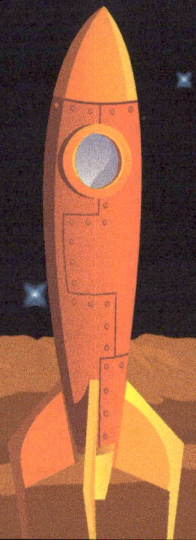

The soil can be used to grow food as well, once some of the toxic chemicals have been removed and it's been supplemented with the nutrients that plants need.

Mars

Mars

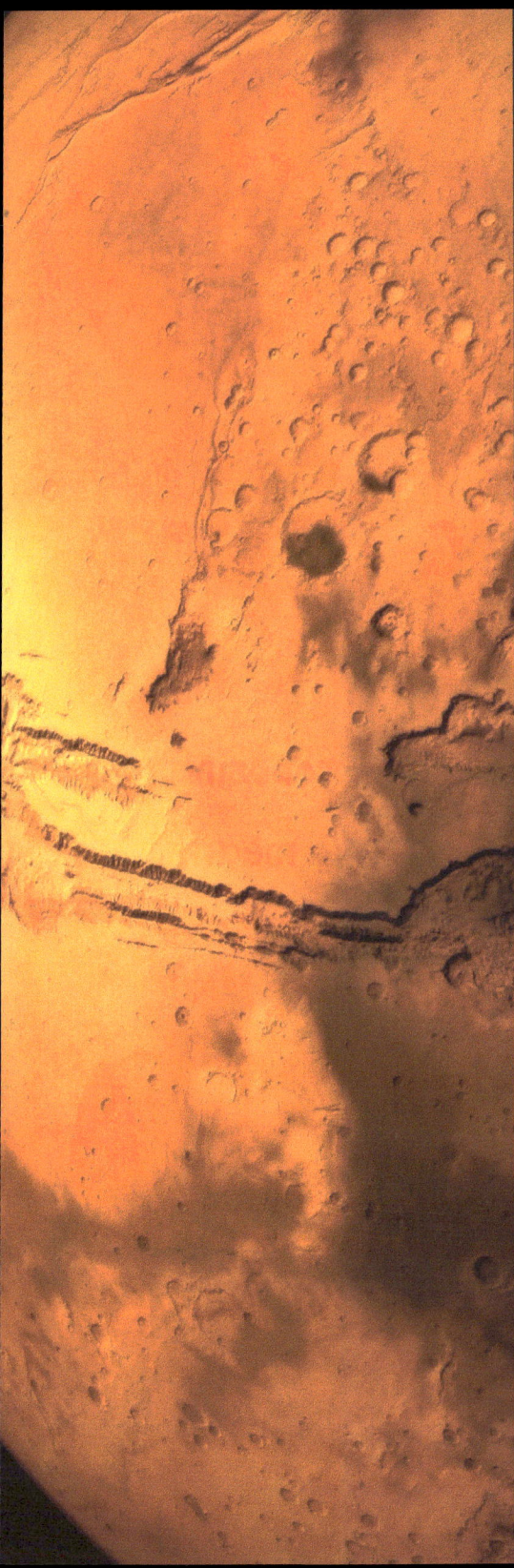

Over time it might be possible for humans to change their own biology through genetic engineering so that future humans could survive and thrive in the conditions that already exist on Mars. Plants and animals could also be genetically engineered to adapt more readily to the conditions on Mars.

TERRAFORMING

For decades, science fiction writers have been proposing the idea of "terraforming" Mars. Terraforming means manipulating a planet to deliberately make it more Earthlike so that people can eventually live there.

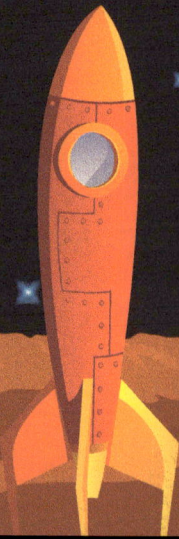

Mars

All sorts of interesting and elaborate ideas have been proposed for solving the problems on Mars and converting it into a "second Earth." Science fiction is frequently ahead in describing advances in technology that may not occur for hundreds if not thousands of years.

It seems ironic that with all the problems we have with Earth's climate and other environmental issues that some scientists still believe that Mars could be shaped to become an ideal second Earth. Even without any grass on the surface of the planet, it seems that the "grass is greener" on Mars than it is on our own planet!

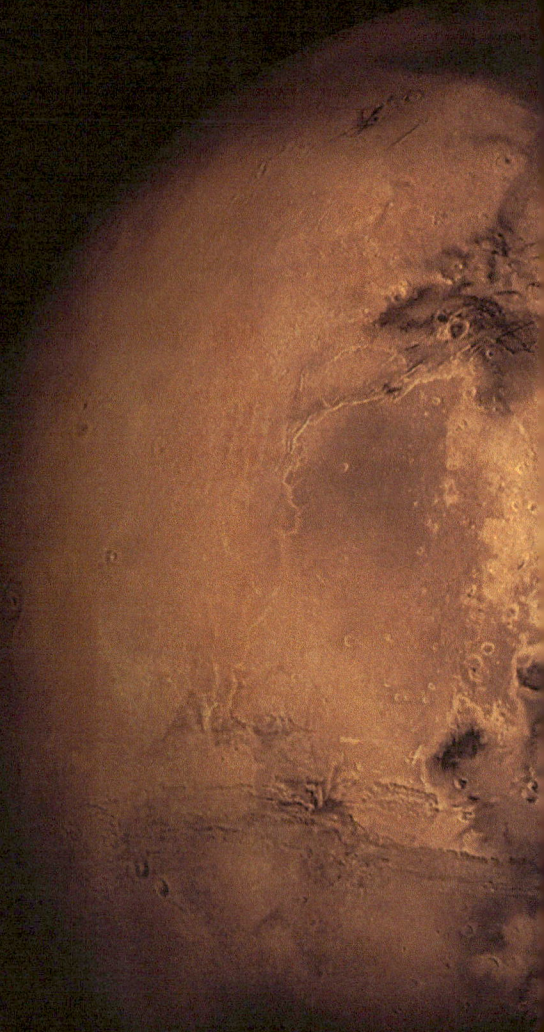

Mars

Planet Mars

The "greening" of Mars would require that we bombard it with tons and tons of greenhouse gases to warm it up. This would melt the frozen water, which would provide the needed nourishment to grow plants. Eventually, as it happened on Earth, plants would take in carbon dioxide and give off oxygen, thus creating an atmosphere.

While all this is going on, some scientists have suggested that the planet should be encapsulated in a giant dome. Once the atmospheric pressure and the contents of the atmosphere are correct for humans to survive and thrive, then the dome could be removed!

Planet Mars

Planet Mars

It sounds feasible, but it's so much easier said than done. We might have to do some demolition using the power of harnessed comets in order to get the needed water and other chemicals required to build on the surface.

HOW LONG WOULD IT TAKE TO TERRAFORM MARS?

It took millions of years for the climate and conditions on Earth to nurture complex forms of life. It's difficult to say how long it would take to terraform a planet like Mars. It's more than likely that it would take thousands if not millions of years for such a transformation to take place.

Consider what happened when Europeans came to the "New World" of North America. Many colonists died and whole colonies were wiped out by disease and the harsh conditions during the winter. All this took place on planet Earth so it's not hard to imagine the difficult realities that the first colonists on Mars will face. It would be surprising if the first colonists survive with few problems.

During the Depression in the United States there was a huge "Dust Bowl." Giant dust storms swept over the land, wiping out any possibility for the growth of crops and causing many people to get sick when the dust got into their lungs. There were also people who went crazy emotionally from the bleak environment during the Dust Bowl.

Mars

Mars

Mars is a barren landscape with a dusty, rocky surface. The soil on Earth is filled with organic matter. It's teeming with both unseen and visible life. A handful of soil from Mars is lifeless as is its surface. We don't have any clue how humans will feel over time when the only life on the surface includes themselves and the few plants and animals they have brought with them.

Despite all these issues, there's a high likelihood that humans will someday form a colony on Mars. All exploration and travel to new frontiers has brought danger and risk to mankind.

Mars

Mars

However, when the challenges have been conquered it has also brought human beings to a new level. Perhaps it's our destiny to travel not only to the planets within our solar system, but to eventually travel to other planets in planetary systems that are light years away from us.

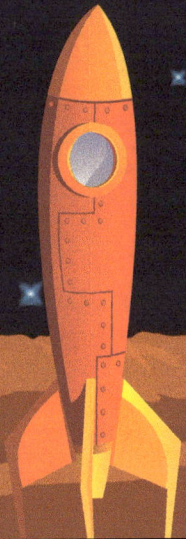

Scientists have devised guidelines to search for these habitable planets as they look to the future. Planets must meet a certain set of criteria to be in the "goldilocks" zone—not too hot and not too cold. They have to be a specific distance from their stars, which are their suns.

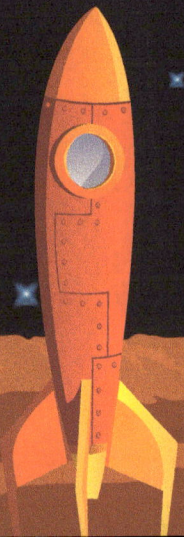

Mars

Mars

They need to have liquid water and an atmosphere that is breathable for humans. Perhaps by the time we have the technology to travel there, we will know how to transform any of the environmental conditions that are less than ideal. Perhaps you'll be a member of the scientific team that gets us there!

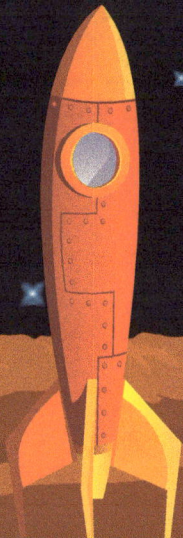

Awesome! Now you know more about whether someday people will colonize Mars. You can find more Astronomy & Space books from Baby Professor by searching the website of your favorite book retailer.

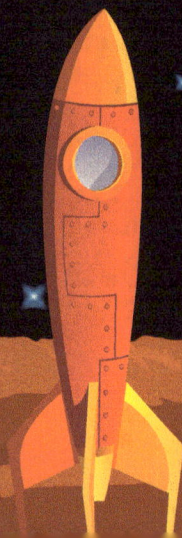

Visit

BABY PROFESSOR
EDUCATION KIDS

www.BabyProfessorBooks.com

to download Free Baby Professor eBooks
and view our catalog of new and exciting
Children's Books

Milton Keynes UK
Ingram Content Group UK Ltd.
UKHW051124030924
447802UK00003B/52

9 798869 415059